THE HABITUAL
PEACEFULNESS
OF GRUCHY

Poems After Pictures by Jean-François Millet

David Middleton

Louisiana State University Press

Baton Rouge

Designer: Laura Roubique Gleason
Typeface: Centaur
Printer and binder: Data Reproductions

LIBRARY OF CONGRESS CATALOGING-IN-PUBLICATION DATA
Middleton, David, 1949–
    The habitual peacefulness of Gruchy : poems after pictures by Jean-François
Millet / David Middleton.
        p.   cm.
    ISBN 0-8071-3081-8 (pbk. : alk. paper)
    1. Millet, Jean François, 1814–1875—Poetry. 2. Painting—Poetry. I. Title.
PS3563.I362H33 2005
811'.54—dc22
                                                        2005015565

A number of the poems in this collection first appeared in the following journals:
*The Anglican, Anglican Theological Review, Chronicles, The Classical Outlook, Desire Street,
Kestrel, Littératures, Histoire des Idées, Images, Sociétés du Monde Anglophone (LISA), Louisiana
Literature, New Compass, New Delta Review, Pivot, POEM, Sewanee Review, Smartish Pace,*
and *South Carolina Review.*

I wish to thank the Division of the Arts of the State of Louisiana for a poetry
fellowship in the summer of 2001, a fellowship which made possible the comple-
tion of some of these poems. In addition, I am grateful to Deborah Cibelli of
the School of Fine Arts at Nicholls State University for matters concerning art
history and the availability of reprints of Millet's pictures. Finally, I remain in-
debted, as always, to Nicholls State University for honoring me with the title of
poet-in-residence and providing support that made possible the composition of
these and other poems.

in memory of
Catherine Lemaire,
Madame J.-F. Millet,
who bore Millet nine children

My goal was to show the habitual peacefulness of Gruchy,
where each act, which would be nothing anywhere else,
here becomes an event.

    —Letter of 20 April 1868, Millet to Théophile Silvestre

    ✻

The epic of the fields
    —Millet on some of his drawings

Holy ground
    —Vincent van Gogh on Millet's paintings

Contents

THE HABITUAL
PEACEFULNESS
OF GRUCHY

Madame J.-F. Millet

Catherine Lemaire [1827–94]
ca. 1848–49

Each long precisest lash, each hooded lid
Protects in downcast eyes a mystery
Whose depths rise sympathetic to pressed lips,
This Breton Mona Lisa's dimpled smile.

You came to him at only seventeen,
Your dark bunned hair undone by pliant hands,
And bore nine sons and daughters twenty years,
Unwed, then wed in law, by church at last.

And though your only photo shows you glum,
Both staring at and past the opened lens,
This portrait, all those paintings, tell much more:
For you're the farm wife pasturing a cow,

Teaching a daughter knitting, shearing sheep,
Washing at dusk in waters of the sun,
A planter tending, gleaner bending down
Gathering field, hearth, garden into one.

Woman Pasturing Her Cow

ca. 1856–57

Too poor to let her cow graze rented ground,
She leads the beast along a public way
To forage tufts beneath its line of trees
Whose stark trunks bar and mark off private land.

There, fecund herds eat grass in solar gold,
The one black bull mounting cow after cow,
A herdsman leaning forward on his staff,
Exhausted by this plenty he defends.

The woman stays beside her single charge—
Gaunt haunches and the marrow-harrowed bone,
The vivid ribs and skin like fleshly bellows—
And does not gaze upon those Helian fields

But stands erect with staff against her lap,
Knitting between her fertile womb, full breasts
Contented with subsistence like her cow
Cropping in dark by arpents of the sun.

Knitting Lesson I

ca. 1854

Through windowpanes the filtered winter light
Passing over a basket's rumpled yarn
Covers a mother's radiant bent face
Whose cheek and chin rest on her daughter's head.

The young girl holds in small soft awkward hands
Long knitting needles glinting in the threads
Looped round a knuckle, woven, then pulled tight,
Part of a garment shadowed in her lap.

With palms grown rough in mastering her craft
The mother, from behind, now clasps and guides
The tender pale pink fingers through their task,
Both bracing and embracing as the dusk

Gathers the light from bonnet, coat, and skirt
That muffle intensest women who themselves
Pull wool from sheep to card, then spin and knit
Into the well-made garments of their lives.

Shearing Sheep

1852–53

A green tree shears the dusky sun in half
Before a thatched stone barn and open hut
Under whose hill of drying, settled grain
A sheep is held and clipped on a barrel top.

The woman, young, well-muscled, bends and snips,
Her free hand braced in clutching uncut curls;
Meanwhile, an older man in peasant blue,
Grimacing, grasps the sheep's feet two by two.

The flock press their wet noses through the bare
Slats of gates where the next ewe on its back
Squirms in cold mud with lashed hooves lurching free,
All caught—these beasts and souls—in raw May air

And in an artist's dream of splitting suns
That die in trees, clumped wool, thatch-raftered grain
And fixed tellurian laborers who stay
Stray solar ghosts chthonian to the bone.

Washerwomen

ca. 1855

The sun still cleans its sky with parting light
Reflected in a pond though pond and sky
Turn turquoise now in evening's spreading stains.
Between them both a long green bank divides

The waters of the heavens and the loam,
Its strip of grass and clay floating amid
This earth and that unearthly realm of stars
Whose arras decks a grove of trees and homes.

By water's edge two washerwomen work
With things wrung free awhile of dirt and sweat,
One bent beneath her burden, hand on hip,
The other gently loading on the clothes.

Soon night will wash faint sunlight from the stars,
The dredger pole his high-piled boat toward shore
To raise a sinking house on sand whose grains
No one can scrub from nothing's cloak of stone.

Potato Planters

1861–62

The plot is small, a patch of ocher-browns
Adorned by kingly purples where a man
Digs out a row of holes in which his wife
Drops seed potatoes from a white cloth sack.

Beyond them, Chailly plain, that vast expanse
Of green and yellow grasses, fertile herds,
And in between the plot and plain, two trees
Whose yellows, greens, and browns unite the scene.

The trees bring gifts of coolness, quiet, and shade
To a basket's dreaming child where watchful eyes
Of a donkey seem to almost comprehend
This infant still asleep in Bethlehem.

The planters' clothes are streaked with clinging earth
That yields a crop some scorn as human food,
But not this family, poorer than the ground,
Their hunger numb to beauty's ocher-browns.

The Gleaners

ca. 1857

Two women bend, a third strains, back half-bowed,
Searching for stalks in well-picked-over fields,
Their meager gleanings clutched to spine, knee, thigh,
Leavings strewn in stubble on this shorn ground.

Paid peasants in the distance thresh and bale
The wheat and hay where a horsed overseer
Directs his laborers by voice or hand,
Boaz remote from these three silent Ruths

Or, more so, the Fates, stark daughters of Night,
Allotters whose dark word destines the child,
Who spin cut hay or wheat in auric weave,
Birth-spirits, from the Second Empire born.

In early drawings, they bow down toward us,
And children bind black sheaves in gay bouquets
While far carts, weighed with grain, are brought so near
We all must breathe the fatal golden dust.

Bust of a Female Nude

ca. 1847–50

Not any nude, but Catherine, we think,
Sometime between nineteen and twenty-three,
Model, or inspiration at the least,
In Paris or your exile's Barbizon.

We see you with your worn black crayon raised
To lift up from flat paper rounded breasts,
Sleek muscled arms, taut belly, and a face
Held fast by pure detachment and desire.

And so we sketch a scene in dusk's spent light,
Catherine's wrap descending from her hips,
Your dusty chalk-stub put aside at last,
The studio abandoned for the bed.

And there she draws you down to what you'd drawn,
A woman flush beyond your crayon's art,
Now coaxing you to be a man alone
And know her in the mortal flesh apart.

In the Garden

ca. 1860

A garden dug in Barbizon—Millet's?—
Late spring or early summer it would seem,
Green sprouts from carrots, onions, beets, and beans
Maturing by the headed lettuce leaves.

Two children still in Eden find themselves
Either side of a twisted cedar tree.
The toddler waves a stick at hungry hens
Poised at the very edge of her domain.

The elder, twelve, leans back against the trunk,
Her hands doing the mending while her eyes
Stare far beyond squat beehives side by side
Whose stings and honey mark the garden's end.

Beside the girl a plain brown basket spills
Bunched linen like the horn of plenty's fruit.
She peers at clouds that soon will bring a rain
Of Adam's sweat and Eve's maternal tears.

Newborn Lamb

1866

The swung-back gate leans still against its hedge
Whose shrubs curl in a tangled darkened arch
Through which a girl bears off a tiny lamb
Before a flock led by the mother ewe.

The ewe's raised head strains up to touch her young
But the girl, gazing downward, swings away,
Cradling between her breasts and aproned womb
The warm new life that fell in meadow grass.

The shepherdess is lost in mother dreams
Though she is but thirteen and does not see
By path-side rocks the spiny yellow furze
Whose thorns prick hungry sheep that eat its leaves.

A pastoral scene from Millet's Norman home
Where his dead sister Emélie could dwell,
Here is no lamb stillborn, no mounting ram,
But gates of life refined in soft pastels.

Little Goose Girl

1868

Perched on a bank whose meadow-grass gives way
To reeds and woody limbs of toughened shrub,
The peasant child, well fed, surveys her realm,
Her first job almost one with make-believe.

Ducks waddling on a path turn verdant heads
Ruled by her limp green branch whose shriveled leaves
Are fluttering just enough to shoo them down
To cool pond water sloshing on the sand.

The meadow crests in barn and farmhouse stone
Sedate between great swathes of sky and grass.
And there, contented geese grow fat on roots,
Then come to bathe and wallow in the wet.

This place, if east of Eden, cannot be
Removed by more than one or two degrees
Of swaying shades of overgrowth whose sheen
Startles the birds and girl from dream to dream.

Goose Girl Bathing

ca. 1863

Late morning and secluded in the cool
Of May's green banks and boughs, this hidden stream,
A girl perhaps fifteen sheds all her clothes,
Then rests beside the waters where she'll bathe.

Her geese and ganders paddle in the wet
Where she as yet but dips one ankle in,
Her gangling body rounding out in soft
Womanly contours—thighs, hips, belly, breasts.

She's been the family goose girl thirteen years
And knows her time as such is near its end.
Between the trees of life and innocence
She stares at her reflection's steady change.

Above her, in dense foliage, two white cows
See all that young men soon will vie to see:
Flesh warming toward its noon in rose and blue,
Those filtered sun-shafts rippling in the depths.

Madame J.-F. Millet

Pauline-Virginie Ono [1821–44]

1841

He painted her for nothing but her love,
A Cherbourg tailor's daughter without means
For such a tender rendering as this:
Desirous, tense, yet teasingly serene,

Those earth-brown irises, that slightest smile,
Hair clipped, severe, tied in a ribboned cap,
The look of expectation, quiet surprise
Directed at this man her brother knew

Who stroked her with his oils and darkened eyes
Until she came alive on canvas threads
That held her there as in her wedding bed.
And though she soon would pass beyond recall

Like those two fruitless, brief Parisian years,
Millet remembered, kept till his own death
This image both relinquished and possessed:
And Catherine saw them kiss through widow's tears.

The Lovers

ca. 1848–50

An oval cameo with bank and tree
Frames nothing else but this most secret scene:
Two faces blurred as mind drifts into sense,
Flesh waking to its latent ecstasy.

His left hand from behind holds her left breast,
His right hand stilled for now beside her crotch,
His muscled back and buttocks, bulging thighs
Ready to root him soon in softest earth.

Venus and Adonis? Adam and Eve?
Old Master precedents or peasants glimpsed?
All these perhaps yet we guess something more
Hearing a Breton housemaid's climbing cries,

She who would heal him of his first wife's death—
Tubercular Pauline who bore no child—
Spreading her legs to let her belly swell
When soul and phallus spilled their pent-up seed.

Woman Sewing Beside Her Sleeping Child

ca. 1858–62

An inner twilight deepens in the room:
The smoky oil lamp pegged high on its stand,
A child tucked-in beneath the blanketing beams,
The shadowed mother mending in her chair.

She pulls a woolen thread to close a seam
In the work shirt of a father still afield
Plowing his darkened rows until the stars
Gleam twinkling from the yielding fertile earth.

Behind the smoke that clusters into curls
A bed whose drapes recall a garden wall
Awaits her strong young husband and the night,
Her warm wet furrow eager for his seed.

The child will never waken from its bed,
The mother never finish like Millet
Who made of color-threads this scene he dreamed
Between the twilight times of dusk and dawn.

Faggot Gatherers on the Edge of Fontainebleau Forest

ca. 1850

They came when he had laid his brushes down,
Light passing from the palette and his face
As evening drew him near the forest's edge
To be at peace among his painted scenes.

But seated under finished winter trees
Whose wild fall fruit had fed both life and art
He soon saw limbs move stiff through Fontainebleau,
Huge bundled faggots bending backs and legs

Of stick-like human figures, crayon-gray,
Old women, men, the poorest of the poor
Gathering sheaves to stave off death with fire.
And when at last sheer pity took them in

Not as mere subjects for his craft but souls
Bearing the common burdens of this earth
He thought of one whose eyes, when half-repaired
By miracle, had seen men walk like trees.

Entrance to the Forest at Barbizon in Winter

1866–67

No springtime cows, heavy with milk or young,
Now pass the ancient gate to graze on grass
Beyond this wall of beeches dense and deep
Where birds peck up the snowflake-crusted seeds.

One stone gatepost remains, the other gone
Or crumbled into rubble in the drift
Where siftings upon siftings blow through trees,
Old matter's ghostly soul that roams the earth.

The beeches' topmost boughs branch up in V's
Outreaching to embrace down-gliding birds
Whose V-winged shapes alight on kindred limbs
Above the forest's darkened common ground.

The trees speak in a language all their own
Known only to interpreters, the birds,
Who leave their runic footprints in the snow
Before tall beeches standing there like runes.

Farmyard by Moonlight

1868

A full moon under tattered, speckled clouds
Shines down upon a courtyard where a dog
Stares back at glowing stone, yet hardly more
Aware of it than it has been of him.

The moonlight spills through gate-slats to the mud
Where a wheelbarrow with its load of sticks
Seems far from labors done or still to do.
A puddle's tufts take root in lunar seas.

Outside the yard a dead tree's scraggly limbs
Grasp ragged clouds and claw up to the moon
That stays above some central place unseen
Beyond the courtyard's blocking granite walls.

And here, though silence listens, no one states
Its blatant implications that surround
The barrow, dog, tuft-puddle, gate, and tree
Eternal in their mortal light and dark.

Landscape with Shepherdess and Sheep, Winter

ca. 1850–52

Her back against a talus topped with trees
Whose new-growth leaves and limbs have long been stripped
High as a sheep can reach, bare as her staff,
She seems as sheer and stiff as bank and trunk.

Her long plain dress and face, cape, hood, and shoes
Emerge from wastes surrounding Barbizon,
This over-cropped and well downtrodden turf,
Grim given no skilled rendering dispels.

A fallen branch lies blanched as cattle bones.
Two ewes snuggle for warmth where no grass grows.
Others pull crusted roots up where the sun
Grazes in winter dusk on frozen dew.

A draftsman mastering what he loved and knew,
First fully realized here in theme, technique,
He sensed at last his art's profoundest ground,
The pastoral raised to epic dignity.

Path Through the Wheat

ca. 1867

The hillside's tidal waves of yellow-green
Break downward into full-grown stalks of wheat
In which a peasant, shouldering his hoe,
Passes along a snaking narrow path—

A teeming place through which his hard thighs press
And where his head just barely stays above
The swaying grain, drunken in abundance,
Farm buildings almost floating on the swells

Beyond which sea gulls gliding white in air
Fly down on out of sight to salty fields,
Taking the channel fish off Normandy,
A surfeit fit for Eden in its dawn.

Yet as the peasant moves through such high grass
Made edible in bread he will in time
Stumble upon a skull from Arcadie,
Abel's cranium anchoring the grain.

The Sower

1850

He strides with massive thighs and torso turned
Like Michaelangelo's Adam now combined
At last with the Apollo Belvedere,
This Norman peasant scattering the corn

On broken hillside ground as twilight fails.
He binds his calves with straw against the cold,
Sowing winter wheat in mid-November,
The earth disturbed again by human need.

Upon the furrowed crest a harrow dragged
By huge white oxen covers up the seed
While birds descend, black-winged, from threatening skies
To feed upon some gleaming unturned grains.

His clothes are red and blue, his eyes unseen
Beneath his low-brimmed hat, his look intent,
Inscrutable in fearful dignity,
Mysterious with life's prime mystery.

Two Men Turning Over the Soil

1866

They work upon the untilled hillside soil,
Rocky and uneven, all splotched with tufts
Of green and yellow grasses stark in March,
Shovels cutting and dumping lumps of earth

While in the golden distance plains seem set
For planting furrows streaked bright pink and blue,
Small piles of fired weeds making pure white smoke,
Some great estate long settled in its ways.

The father frowns and stares at bare turned ground
Beside his son who uproots turf observed
By eyes more full of wonder than despair
From those few springtime years he's labored there.

These are the priests whose solemn, common mass
Will raise up grape and grain from canvas-clays
Blocked out by Millet's crayons and pastels,
His stippled sweat saltwatering the rocks.

Buckwheat Harvest

1868–70

The ground is Norman—windswept coastal soil
As thin as seed-and-harvest time is short,
Too poor for oxen trampling out the grain
And yet a place where hardy buckwheat grows.

In stubble, bent-backed women bind and tie
The pink-white clustered flower-heads in shocks,
Then shoulder them or push square-basket sleds
Toward circled threshers raising up dead limbs.

Like some archaic pagan sacrifice,
Men thrash split stalks and chaff to free the seed.
One with a pitchfork tosses straw on fire
Whose winnowed smoke spreads high in cirrus skies.

The church in distant Gruchy's barely seen
Between these gatherings of germ and cloud,
Its steeple pitched, a shock of headed stone
To rocky backs that bow toward toil alone.

Harvesters Resting

1853

The pink and golden graindust spreads its mist
Glittering over the reapers' spare noon meal—
Water from red-brown pots of earthenware,
Mush that crude spoons scoop from a common bowl.

And while they sit or sprawl by wheat stacks swelled
Like many-breasted Cybele, one stands,
The scythers' overseer, whose arms link them
And a gleaner-girl come shy in Virgin-blue.

The tale is Ruth and Boaz now transposed
From Bethlehem to France's central plain
With Boaz no rich kinsman but the same
As these he drives for absent heirs abroad.

Though foreign, Ruth will find a husband here
And bear the common realm inside her womb,
A Moabite at home in Israel,
Ancestress and descendent of its kings.

Gleaner Returning Home with Her Grain

ca. 1857–62

No blissful gleaner dreamed by Jules Breton
With bundled grain raised high on slender arms—
A beauty fleeing wheat fields for the town—
But one near such, in twilight left behind.

Her sheaf is balanced on her head by palms
And elbows crooked to bear her gatherings.
Beyond her, dusk's last harvesters still strain
To rake up, then haul off the fallen stalks.

Nearby, two plainer women lag behind,
Bundles shouldered or held by low-locked hands,
Climbing under a new moon's crescent rim,
A disc wedged bright in scattered ash of clouds.

The first girl's tucked-up skirt, bared petticoat,
Strong arms, broad haunches, modest ready breasts
Tell us she'll stay and be some farmer's wife
Gleaned from the leavings of her class and sex.

Return of the Flock

ca. 1863–64

Across the blue horizon that divides
Pale twilight skies from twilight-darkened earth
A shepherd leads beneath a crescent moon
His bending line of pliant moon-eyed sheep.

The laggards and the leaders, nipped by dogs,
Swirl from a formless mass of flesh and wool
Toward faces separated yet the same,
Soon lost to sun in starlight like the stars.

The shepherd in procession grasps his staff,
His right hand parting a cloak to show within
The long blue shirt, a bishop's under-robe,
Literal symbols speaking for themselves.

Both moon and flock are turning toward their homes.
This shepherd is his sheep's blind overseer.
His sheepdogs push and lead the column on
Till shepherd, prelate, moon, and flock are one.

Killing the Hog

ca. 1867–70

The painting is unfinished, rightly so,
For it depicts what never has an end:
A fat hog on her haunches pushed and drawn
Out of the barn to this small walled-in place,

Two men pulling a rope tied round the snout,
And a woman coaxing, showing the beast
A bucket's tilted lip of slop and corn,
November's emblem, bleak with our bleak need.

The hog has caught the scent of other hogs
On the butcher's stained apron and she squeals
So near the slaughter-board, the primal scene,
The long knife and the basin for the blood.

Huddled and wrapped against a wall and cold,
Two ghostly children—charcoal, not pastel—
Appalled yet famished, fix on death and ham,
This open abattoir, hunger's great I AM.

Bird Trapper

1867

The artist sets us here in this dark barn
Directed by perspective through a door
Opening on a yard now cloaked with snow
Where a propped shutter shades new-sprinkled seed.

Hard by the door a kneeling trapper peers
Along his stringy rope tied to a stick
Holding its shutter up above a bird
That takes from flakes this windfall autumn grain.

Beyond the trap and snow-topped garden wall
Warier birds watch from a leafless tree;
Others, foolish and lucky, walk the edge
Of boards that drop and smash one unaware

When a trickster yanks and the prop-stick flies,
The shutter crushing feather, beak, and skull
To add to a winnowing basket's limp heap
Of flesh well-fed on manna and the Fall.

The Winnower

ca. 1847–48
 for J.A.C.

Threshed wheat now rests in mounds where sackcloth frays
Threading in dark above a framework shed
Down channel winds that salt well-sweetened seed
A winnower tosses from his tight-weave scoop,

Grain beaten from light chaff that's swept a-breeze
Powdering yellow swells like stellar dust.
Beyond this unwalled hut far stars remain,
Sifted from drifts of chaos and the night,

Grist milled for heaven's bread, an astral staff
Risen from germs that spurn their dusky husks,
The wrenched essentials' dreaded separations
In fluted marrow's windblown bone and soul.

Implicit in this local Norman scene,
Such castings up of dross-and-gold sew winds
That loop and lash where flaring ashes fare:
The Winnower's Scoop, but woven of the air.

Peasant and Donkey Returning Home at Dusk

ca. 1866—68

Between raised ochre plains and low slate skies
Pressing against stray clustered tufts of trees
A tapered wedge is driven blue through light
Flaring from clouds that tatter in the air.

And on a scarred black path that blindly winds
Unoutlined at the utmost edge of dusk
A peasant, brown and dark on dark brown earth,
Draws his tired donkey, burdened in the murk.

Cross-hatched, then rubbed and blended, well-stumped lines
Show sun-flecks streaming home from cloud and plain,
Escaping wraiths both radiant and grave,
Brightness incised, fleeing a bleak demesne.

These winter rows are sown with dusk and cold.
This man has bound and baled late wheat and hay,
Surd stalks fettered and pressed in night's blind vise,
Words stark as their unlettered dark and day.

Man with a Hoe

ca. 1863

He leans on the short handle, knotted oak,
Its flat blade pressed on brambled clay and stone.
A boulder shoulders thorns up from the soil
While oxen plow a far-off pastoral farm

Whose stubble-fires smoke white toward skies in haze.
He dominates the land as serf and lord,
The subject monarch of his stark domain,
His thistle-crown root-bound in freehold earth.

Not fallen from some paradise whose crops
Turned golden while he plucked a harp's ripe strings,
He's come down long hard centuries the same,
Man's bent-back state no revolutions change.

Millet made no more gestures after this
But concentrated on technique alone,
Placing his faith in color, shape, and line
To render such grim dignity divine.

Winter Evening

1867

A single oil lamp, hanging like a star,
Shines from its pole down on the hooded crib
Whose infant sleeps deeper than night and day.
His face unseen, the husband, with skilled hands

Weaves reeds into a basket like the one
Near him holding tools—chisels, mallets, awls?—
Employed through winter sabbaths from the work
That binds his sweat and seed to Adam's earth.

Beside his stool his wife sews in a chair,
Mending some plain white garment thread by thread.
Her full pink blouse and gray-green skirt reveal
A body fit to bear a farmer's sons.

What lies outside this Norman Nazareth
The fireside cat that stares at flames recalls:
Snow filling darkness with its cold white glow,
Each flake unique and common in its fall.

Watering Horses: Sunset

1866

Flared light in the dimming center radiates
Between low pink or higher turquoise clouds
And sundown browns that cloak the winter Seine,
Soaking its banks' dead sedge near Barbizon.

A peasant riding bareback on a mare
Leads other tired draft horses down to drink
From waters crimped and furrowed like the fields
In which they left their lather's salty seed.

The rider tugs the heavy wingless beasts
Into their own reflections unaware
Of anything outside this thirsty dark,
Their history, like their lives, a twilight scene.

Such figures drift upriver with the night
Toward dawn-times when great Pegasus a-wing
Would fly pink-turquoise skies, then glide on light
To lap his bright face up from pastoral streams.

Farmyard in Winter

1868

From low gray skies slow streams of moistened snow
Whiten stiff limbs leaden above a hutch
Where fattened hens and cocks stay quiet and still.
Meanwhile, outside, on crusted sheaves and stones

Wild birds alight to search out frozen grain,
Including one chill robin, perched, alert
Between the thatch-roofed chickens and the rooks
That sink down in a drizzle-glaze bone cold.

Below a smoldering chimney's topping-snow
A single hen, venturing from the rest,
Pecks lean gleanings under the flakes' bright pall,
Her crest and robin redbreast flush with want.

What farm folk do inside the distant house
Is unexpressed, though through the chimney-keep
Smoke slips from fires whose silent tongues caress
Baked chicken, apple brandy, sex, and sleep.

Twilight

1859–63

The sun's failing radiance draws the moon
Out of that dark a foreign light defines
In crescents which embrace its dusty stone
Reigning over the brown unplanted plain.

The cloaked wife on a donkey, unsold sheep
Returning from the market to their fold,
The husband on foot—a holy family
Going toward Egypt or toward Bethlehem?

No, here's no Joseph with some sheltered flock,
No Norman pastures greening channel cliffs
With heads of wheat tossed in the salted air,
No fig or grape to pluck from limb or vine

But bleak and unalleviated ways
Between the market cross and stark despair,
Blank cravings just to eat and sleep and be
In twilights of the cosmos and their lives.

Woodcutter Making a Faggot

ca. 1853–54

Cold light above leaves his grim face in shade
As does a hat whose pulled-down brim half hides
Eyes focused on the task: lopping off shoots
From branches on a tripod cutting-stump.

Before him lie more branches still to trim,
Beside him a crude-fashioned faggot-crib,
Behind him great bound stacks of bundled sticks,
Beyond him, dense and endless, Fontainebleau.

His work is also endless, bill-hook raised,
Then dropped to chop away dry sprouted twigs
Until the winter dusk's stark frost and dark
Grant timeless labor temporary rest.

The bare embankment swells toward huddled trunks
Awaiting bleaker winters yet untold
When even trees of knowledge and of life
May yet be felled to burn in utmost cold.

Cooper Tightening Staves on a Barrel

ca. 1848–52

His mallet raised again to strike a wedge
Forcing stretched vine-hoops down to brace the staves
And make oak barrels watertight for wine,
The cooper finds the rhythm of his craft.

The barrel rises higher than his eyes
That stare through his own cast shadow at the task
As though he nailed a silhouette on wood:
His artisan's blue tunic black with blood.

The worker and his work are all but one,
Descended from Burgundian books of hours
Through almanacs to picture magazines,
An emblem of September's ripened vines

For him who by the strokes of his poised brush
Raised up this mallet made of ink and oil
While wine-drunk craftsmen, come from Gothic stone,
Staggered across the Paris barricades.

Training Grape Vines

ca. 1860–64

The dresser weaves spring trellises with vines
Whose leaves and tendrils sprout out opposite
With each fifth tendril flaring into flowers
That bear black grapes for dry red autumn wines.

He bends away from ochre-shadowed grass
Toward ancient fruit-trees twisted like the shrubs
Either side of a lichened garden wall
Beyond which slopes his tilled and seeded field,

A ridge of stiff, still beeches without leaf,
And skies whose blue the clouds turn white and gray.
Above the wall pink petals seem to dance
Free of their limbs and trunks, a powdered paste

Of matter that no underlaid black sketch,
No Dionysus, Eostre, Christ the vine
Sustains as well as well-trained grapes persist
In making raisins, vinegar, and wine.

Woman Baking Bread

ca. 1852–56

She leans back, hunches forward, as she shoves
Over the baked-brick oven's steady flames
The long peel with its spade-head's puffed-up dough,
Her strained arms browned and muscled like a man's.

Green wheat made ripe and gold in solar winds,
Its threshed grain milled by grinding stone on stone,
Warm-water yeast cakes melting into foam—
These mix with milk and sugar kneaded in.

No longer hunter-gatherers who once
Plucked woodland fruit or brought down mastodons,
We tend our fathers' orchards, fields, and folds
Not for unleavened bread in exodus

Or doorways washed with blood or tempting loaves
Conjured from rock or in an upper room
But just for strength to push the yeasty seed
Into the rising wetfires of the womb.

Young Woman Churning Butter

ca. 1848–51

Her eyes turned down, absorbed by what she does,
Strong arms stirring the churn-stick in the churn
Over and over and over till cream
Makes butter from its water, fat, and air,

She labors as a Norman peasant would
Not for herself but others far away
In Paris restaurants and dining rooms
Where chilled squares melt on bread their *fleurs-de-lis.*

Yet here, in weary anonymity,
A woman works and works the buttered cream
In utter resignation, tired and bored,
Left in a world whose elements congeal

Those old emulsions mixed with grace and fate,
The curse of Adam fixed in her drawn face,
The black background, the shelf of waiting jugs
She rose at one o'clock to fill by dawn.

Morning Toilette

ca. 1860–62

Through diamond panes webbed tight in crosshatched lead
Pale strands of morning's pliant light are strained,
Falling so soft on cheeks that none can see,
Obstructed by an upper arm and hand—

A harvest-girl just risen from her bed.
The rumpled single sheets, a pillow pressed,
Are wet with unkissed tears. The filtered beams
Reveal a pitcher, crumpled cloth, wood comb

Distilled upon the sill in gold and blue.
This is a private moment unconfined
By role or sex, unvexed and intimate,
The hidden inwardness that all possess.

And yet since there's no husband and no child
To call her wife and mother she must work
Into a knotted bun those gathered strands
That none caress, locks strained against the grain.

The Departure

ca. 1858—62

The solid granite farmhouse stands behind
A backyard garden where bright flower beds
Might well have thrived had not necessity
Demanded rows of shallots, cabbages

And carrots by an open-top Dutch door
Through which a father bends to work in dark.
Outside, walking a furrow-halving path,
A woman holds a basket and her child

Who reaches toward a hidden warm fresh loaf,
Intelligence and hunger meshed in flesh.
The mother's soft sage whispers curb the hand
Of one bundled in bonnet, dress, and cloak,

Conceived on sheets now drying on the slats
Of a picket fence that marks this fruitful yard
The girl must leave to bargain in the town
For rinds that once held seeds of paradise.

Peasant Children at a Goose Pond

ca. 1865–68

Her bent knee on a fence's lower pole,
Plump elbows on the upper in its notch,
A leafy reed her rod, the watchful child
Seems poised between the realms of work and play.

Her brother with his palms pressed flat on grass,
His back against an unforbidden tree,
Gazes on geese that take the worn brown path
To eat wild greens, then lap their splashings up.

Above deep banks of water, shade, and rock
The plowed spring ground awaits its maiden buds.
A worn-out mother leads two cows between
The seeded rows and homes of thatch-roof stone

Sinking amid the wrinkled fields and sea.
The Norman woman looks down on her young
Who wonder at these geese that preen and breed,
Then drift on the stilling ripples of the pond.

Motherly Precaution

1862

Translated onto glass from copper plates,
As from Rembrandt or Brueghel or their heirs,
In whose busy depictions such an act
Is incidental, some side-alley fact,

Now placed here in the center by Millet—
This all-too-human scene, both rude and true:
A mother wrinkling up her young son's gown
Before he wets himself on backdoor steps

Where his six-year-old sister, shrinking, stares
At the wobbly colossus, wholly exposed.
His soft hand grips his mother's muscled wrist,
Still nearer to the milked than milky breast

That manly hands will master, hard and warm,
Till old age brings him trembling to a crone
Who'll lead to darkened doorway-stones once more
This human flesh incontinent with need.

Shepherdesses Watching a Flight of Wild Geese

1866

Sheep graze along a plain in twilight quiet,
Their earthward heads cropping dark clumps of grass,
And near them, by a hedge where yellow leaves
Grow golden in the evening's mellowed air,

Bent over yarn and needles knitting wool
From these same sheep for mittens—two young girls.
Then suddenly one rises, shades her eyes
And gestures to the other not to move,

One arm crooked and one stretched out like the V's
Of geese intent on their archaic way
Beyond the late fall cold toward Galilee.
The one who stands leaves raveled knitting spilled,

But she who sits and leans back on the hedge
Holding the needlework she'll soon complete
Appears the more enraptured in her gaze,
Eros sublimed and climbing toward the sun.

Flight of Crows

ca. 1866

Their feathers lift them high through feathery trees
Tall, thin, and almost leafless far in fall
Before a small mauve pond from which the birds
Drink till startled, then scatter toward the clouds,

Their bent wings flapping black in blackened skies.
The sun arcs down below its curving earth
That crests in the wide rough plains near Barbizon.
A golden glow illumines as it fades.

Some landless peasant girl leading her cows
To feed between the cultivated fields
Stands with an arched back, steadied by a staff,
Watching crows leave the screening trees and glide

There in the middle distance where the air
Holds clay and flame and water till the dusk
Concedes these plains to darkness and its stars,
Those fire birds bright against the night's vast pond.

Shepherd Minding His Sheep

ca. 1863–66

This weathered wall that separates the plain
From forest when Chailly meets Barbizon
Is now itself divided where a path
Brings sheep between its crumbling, grassy stones.

They leave the baking orange sky and fields
Of high-stacked hay, the shepherd's picket-fold
For pastureland this side of fallen rocks,
Tall blades so green and cool in shade that spreads

From trees, which, undepicted, must be there
Behind our set perspective on the scene.
Some ewes crop roots while others nudge and bleat.
One lifts her head, impatient, wedged behind

Slow sisters nearing Canaan's verdant ground.
Atop the wall, the shepherd looks and broods
Like Moses on Mount Nebo, gazing down,
Amazed at deprivation's plenitude.

Watering Cows

1863

The moon's curved rim of pale reflected light
Shines blindly down on sheepdog, shepherd, sheep,
And on a cowherd with her stick to make
Slow cows drink up the rippling lunar gleams.

The flock heads toward a dense green clump of trees
Just past the far bank, Eden's final stand,
Protected, as we see it, by a stream
Flowing between its origin and end.

This side, the cows, whose milk, skin, blood, and meat
We feast upon and wear, move through the world,
Unmindful of their deaths, of drying hides
Or stench of entrails rent from roasted flesh.

Yet here as well the cowherd's rich pink vest
Sustains pure light and color as the west
Spreads everywhere its hueless gloom until
All colors fade in dusk's pervasive gray.

End of the Hamlet of Gruchy (II)

1866

The last house, made of granite, flowering slate,
Now shades a mother's chair and spinning wheel
Abandoned to the geese and afternoon's
Deep peace in which a restless child is held

Up close to a contorted cliffside elm
Whose roots clutch hard the stony Norman soil
Where stunted trunk and lashed limbs imitate
The primal clash of fire, earth, water, air.

The village lives in quiet. A single cry
Of goose or duck or gull is local news
Replete with common portents quickly grasped
As when the hind goose turns half toward the child

Who feels the elm's rough bark with softest hands
That, when the years have toughened them, will reach
In dream toward wind-whipped limbs which at the last
Embrace him in his manhood's spinning end.

Millet's Birthplace in Gruchy

ca. 1863

The chiseled, wedged, and mortared pale red walls
Rise up from granite hardened by those dawns
That stain each shutter, window, porch, and door
Opening on the well-tracked village street.

The stony ruts are furrows where the birds—
Domestic geese and ducks, wild rooks and gulls—
Peck seeds and pull up worms until a wife
Sweeps out dust and ashes over their heads.

Between two doors, one opened and one closed,
A child of seven seems to brace his house,
Hands pressed against recessed and jutting rock
Long settled on the still unsettled earth.

The child has eyes for color, form, design,
And fingertips he'll roughen like a brush
To paint, when deep gray wrinkled brow and brains
And heart and mind combine, these things redeemed.

House with a Well at Gruchy

ca. 1863

The scene is what it was when he was born
Across the street: the deep-dug village well
Protected by its squat turret of rock
Topped by a stone cone cap and rounded knob.

Beside the well, where worn-down stairs meet ground,
A Norman woman in her peasant dress—
White bonnet, blouse, red bodice, full blue skirt—
Feeds geese with bread crumbled from loaves she holds.

The gathered birds soon gulp a puddle up,
Then strut by the granary toward distant pools
Outside the village where they bathe and play
In rains that welled from heaven's fountainhead

Kept pure for those who draw from stellar dells
Or else from clay beneath the deepest graves
Waters that once had rolled through burning foam
Till fire made salt bring crystals from the waves.

Cliffs at Gruchy

1870–71

Downward from Gruchy, past its wind-wrenched elm,
The path drops under pastures to a cliff
Where outcrop boulder-stones glint blue and iron,
Breaking above great sweeps of sea and sky.

Below the rocks, rowing in close to shore
The fishermen, no bigger than the gulls
That turn above them crying at their catch,
Glide over green and lavender to sand.

Outside the scene, a higher, flatter rock
Provided the perspective for these stones
That point toward the horizon's shining line,
Insight's limitless limit bound by sight.

The boulders are an outpost in between
Earth's umbers, turquoise seas, and azure skies,
Distinguished by the mind that from its cliff
Brought fire inside this elevated cave.

Coming Storm

1867-68

Piled up to great black heights like an anvil
Struck by Thor till Viking lightning thundered
On Chailly's plain, cumulonimbus clouds
Roll over seabirds buoyant in the wake.

A farmer far below pulls the unyoked team
Of stout draft horses through the thin green strip
Of common land still his, the turned-up plow
Left out in rows the deluge sweeps away.

A road curves and crests where the torrent pours,
Flooding an unseen slope down which it runs
Like chaos in creation, dust raised up
As ash by the bolting fire's electric jag.

This is the road that toward the coming storm
Of trenches drenched, storm-troopers, blitzkrieg springs
Will lead on from a blasted natural plain
And *Sturm und Drang* to a radiant mushroom rain.

Priory at Vauville, Normandy

1872–74

The coarse and common quartz-and-feldspar stone
Named for its hard grain *granite* dominates
The scene: William the Conqueror's priory
Rising up rock by rock from solid earth.

Abandoned when the guillotine blades fell
On royal and revolutionary necks,
The chapel has no altar candlelit,
No chalice's or paten's elements

Of holy blood and flesh but serves instead
To store a farmer's grain and Christmas wine.
Outside, a peasant leads toward pastured cliffs
White cows he fattens for their milk and meat.

The gate creaks in the worn long-sunken wall
As man and beast move to their given ends.
Nearby, the channel's seagulls search for prey
Above the chapel's crowning salmon arch.

Le Puy du Dôme

ca. 1866–68

These billowing hills crest green in grassy froth
As they have done two thousand years or more
Between some goat-girl and *le Puy du Dôme.*
Older than both the Alps and Pyrenees,

The cone's dark peak is crowned with smoldering clouds
Where radiant glaciations, molten flows
Blazed long ago from *le Massif Central.*
Here goats bed on a precipice or crop

The bedrock's outcrop stone while a girl knits
With legs outstretched, feet splayed, turned well away
From crater lakes and crystalline plateaus.
Her face is featureless, hands indistinct,

Her dwelling brief among these granite swells
Out of the heart of France where basalt veins
Streamed from their peaks when Vercingétorix
Met Caesar on a hill in Burgundy.

Sheepfold by Moonlight

ca. 1856

Low at the dusk's far edge a blunted moon
Descended from its fullness dimly glows.
The night abides again on Chailly plain.
A wandering shepherd labors in faint beams

Till picket-fold and hut rise up once more
From parts kept in a cart that no one sees.
A raised staff comes back down to guide and goad
Each sheep dissolved in darkness and a flock

Shadowed by light but not the source of light.
The bleating of a lost or straggling lamb
Will go unheard in deep exhaustion's sleep,
For here is no Good Shepherd but a man

Staking his claim to rest, then pass away,
His hutch and fence a flimsy citadel
In these Arcadian wastes like Paris, Troy,
Or any other city of the plain.

Young Shepherdess / Captivity of the Jews in Babylon

ca. 1870–73 / 1848
    for Deborah Cibelli, art historian

i.

She sits alone upon a hillock-throne,
Wholly composed of her own history—
The colors of her sculpted woolen skirt
Marbled in knee-splotch greens and blotchy grays,

Her distaff like a queen's rod on her lap
Or lyre wound tight, plucked by the thorny comb,
Her cloud-brimmed hat crowned bright in aureole—
A peasant girl attended by the myths.

And there where rows stream brown away behind
To burst on the horizon white and blue,
Two sheep pause, one haunched up and gazing down
Toward pastureland, the other a blunt head

Rising in dream between the fields and hill,
Almost aware of who this woman is,
The Virgin, Eve, and Ceres of the plain,
Her antique face impassive as a mask.

ii.

And underneath that mask x-rays reveal
To scholars of its art an older tale:
Bearded Assyrian guards whose proffered harps
Make Judah's highborn maidens turn away

In anguish, hiding naked tears that fill
The Tigris and Euphrates with their streams.
No psalms will echo back from garden walls
Where kings hang foreign blooms for foreign wives,

Nor would Millet submit to the Salon
Another many-figured Bible scene,
Only Chailly or his own Normandy
To which the Prussian war exiled him home.

And there, short on supplies, and near the end,
He painted out those maidens for a girl
Whose scepter is the distaff in her palm;
Behind her, Eve, beneath her, Babylon.

Hunting Birds by Torchlight

1874

They make their way by starlight to the trees,
Then light and thrust up torches into limbs
Where settled pigeons stunned with flaring flames
Are bludgeoned by their hundreds to the ground.

Two children fall down scared below a bird
Descending into darkness set ablaze.
One grown-up summons others to the kill.
His helper waves the paralyzing fire.

The earth is full of broken wings and cries,
The flapping back and forth and back again,
Then silence of a fledgling Armageddon,
Creation stained with cruelty, hunger, greed.

Remembered from his childhood near the end
In white and charcoal chalk on rosy gray,
He knew such things had always underlain
The habitual peacefulness of Gruchy.

Self-Portrait

ca. 1840–41

Such portraits in your works are early, rare,
Just two in fact—that Cherbourg fantasy
Tailored to Ono in-laws, white shirt starched,
A black cravat, cheeks shaved like sheep well shorn

And this arch countering image, full rich beard,
High velvet collar, right eye bright, urbane
And frank, the other warier in dark,
Bohemian and peasant, sundered, one—

Yet neither does you justice, your true face
Disclosed in self-effacingness alone,
A model artist modeling on God
Your kingdom ringed by Ptolemaic stars.

And in these poems I've disappeared in you—
Or is it that you've lost yourself in me?—
Our shapes and phrases so alike composed,
Your Channel in the Gulf, my South in Normandy.

The Angelus

1854–59

The Angelus of evening, distant bells,
Three for Ave Marias, versicles,
And nine for every collect low-entoned
By priests inside the far-off village church

Built up from Norman stone. The sky stays gold
Although the sun is gone and shadows pass
Over potato fields where standing still
In attitudes of prayer a man and wife

Think of the Incarnation of their Lord,
The flesh redeemed, a graced creation saved,
Bells pealing from the New Jerusalem
Through history back to Eden's speaking leaves.

Yet here between these dreams of paradise
Potatoes must be planted, tended, dug,
Then sacked on barrows pushed to winter bins
To feast on till the final angels come.